SEA URCHIN
HARAKIRI

To Doctor Eugene Galon
my lost tribe of druidic
know iran-contra heareaganized
echinoids, hoping
he will not
rescue them were
they to choose to
perform their ritual
& theatrical suicide
in his office for its
aseptic & disease-free
environment.

May our brothers in the abysmal
pelagian origin give him an insight
of his hypocondriacopopotamus patient's
brain which tries to reconcile his
psyche with the macro-micro contradic-
-tions & oscillations of our pre-life.

With my gratitude of the Deep for
your friendly & professional care.

Bastille Day
87

BERNARD BADOR

Translation and Introduction

by Clayton Eshleman

Postface by Robert Kelly

Panjandrum Books, Inc.

Los Angeles 1986

Library of Congress Cataloging in Publication Data

Bador, Bernard.
     Sea urchin harakiri.

English and French.
     1. Bador, Bernard—Translations, English.
I. Eshleman, Clayton.   II. Title.
PQ2662.A3236SR   1984   841'.914   84–20637
ISBN 0–915572–77–X
ISBN 0–915572–76–1 (pbk.)

Cover Collage: Bernard Bador
Cover and Book Design: Laurie Haycock

Some of these translations have appeared in the following magazines:
Kayak, Poetry LA, Sulfur, L.A. Weekly, & Conjunctions.

This book was funded in part by a grant from the National Endowment
for the Arts, Literature Program.

Panjandrum Books, 11321 Iowa Avenue, Suite 1, Los Angeles, CA 90025
Manufactured in the United States of America

To Kathryn Lim

TABLE

CONTENTS

INTRODUCTION

Bernard Bador's poetry to date is surely one of the most unique bodies of work to have been influenced by a range of French poetry that begins with Lautremont, passes through Tzara and the various Surrealist strategies of the 20s and 30s, and, for Bador, culminates in the poetry of St.-John Perse. While Bador acknowledges Perse as his most prominent predecessor, in the poetry of the latter it is as if Perse's galleons of light and renewal are suddenly sucked down into the still, black sheen of a petrified whirlpool. Bernard Bador's poetry evokes faceless lakes of stillbeing, grids of flashing lesions, and a garroted apocalypse resplendent with repugnant urges. There is an appetite for slivers here, a special morbidity that recalls the sensibilities of the German poets Georg Trakl and Gottfried Benn (especially the Benn of the lugubrious and slashing *Morgue* poems, where one finds such images as mice building a nest in the belly of a little girl whose murdered corpse was left in a ditch).

If such an image were to appear in a Bador poem, even the consistency of natural disintegration would be warped. The mice might be pregnant with flies, and the little girl, still alive (like one of Hans Bellmer's violated waifs), might be watching the mice, gagged with a cross of excrement. Anticipation of natural event in Bador is always rudely detoured, but at the point that conflicting images start to melt into senselessness, meaning again raises its head, even if wearing its own brain like a perverse tiara.

By locating Bador's writing in a vein that is more Eastern European than French or even German (the world of Vladimir Holan in contrast to that of Paul Eluard), I am actually moving toward the poet's own roots. Bernard Bador is not merely of Hungarian ancestry, but a descendant of the noble Báthory family, which not only included a King of Poland, governors and princes of 16th and 17th century Transylvania, but in those gloomy mountains drained of light from whose folds issued werewolves and mandrakes, the Countess Erzsébet Báthory (1560–1614), a one woman "death camp," who is on record as having hideously tortured and slaughtered over 600 virgins in order to renew her youth by bathing in their blood.[1]

While Bador can hardly be said to have been dominated by a particular ancestor who lived 400 years ago, the coagulated and demonic power in Erzsébet's image appears to have influenced, or flown into, his immediate background so as to affect the nature of his soul, and thus his poetry. I am not one to smirk at the possibility that unappeased, "hungry ghosts" continue to travel the branchings of a family tree until finding a food source, or release, in a particular descendent.

In Bador's poetry at large, and, as I will point out, particularly in his title for this selection, I think it is possible that Erzsébet's seemingly unappeasible hunger for an eroticized mayhem has subsided—as water might in a landscape, leaving the eroded shapes that make up this poetry. Or to put it slightly differently: such hunger has here taken on the form of static, compact stanzas that as their contents are examined begin to resemble plates of cold funereal meats. I can perfectly well imagine Erzsébet's psyche fluttering about these stanzas, nibbling here, sipping there, finding enough death to preoccupy and distract her from what must have seemed to be an endless, ravenous flight through Báthory/Bador progeny.

One reason that I feel this way is that there is no sense of personal experience in Bernard Bador's poetry. The experience is ancestral. Shafts of dusty light reach back to migrations and caravans, to Buddhistic and Hinduistic images, which is to say: a sense of the universe is present. However, it is present as detritus. In contrast to the world of Perse, in which event is always contoured with the rainbow hues of so many stories, in Bador there is incessant entropic closure.

12

Each stanza is an orphan, a little isolated isle, with only possible ties to the one that is found before or behind it. Momentary evocations of grandeur are abruptly doublecrossed by torture, disembowelment, and abortion. Reading him is like watching little pieces being broken off from stories and collaged in such a way that omnipotency and impotency are like grooved pipes that screw into each other perfectly.

What makes these poems unique is the way in which they utilize various Surrealist strategies (especially black humor, Objective Hazard, and the estrangement of sensation) without edging in under the canopy of an established Surrealist voice. The extent to which there is any voice at all is questionable. It might be more accurate to say that these are voiceless, breathless poems, poems in which the words do not seem to be uttered, rhythmless words, words more like bric-a-brac or flea market finds. At the same time these words are highly self-conscious of the way they sound. While poems do "open" and "close," the cuts and cauterizations in discrete stanzas are more significant than any thematic development.

The image of sea urchin harakiri, of a sea urchin inflicting death upon itself, using its spines as medieval Japanese samurai ritually disemboweled themselves, has an odd resonance with one of Erzsébet Báthory's most notorious contraptions, her custom-made clockwork Iron Maiden which she herself designed.

By touching the necklace of encrusted stones that ran in a loop down over the chest, the victim set everything in motion. From the interior of the flesh-color painted iron figure would issue the noise of moving clockwork. Arms would raise and embrace whoever was in reach; where the painted breasts were, two shutters slid sideways, the chest opened, and five daggers slowly emerged, stabbing the girl clasped in the embrace. As other gems in the necklace were pressed, the arms fell away and the eyes clicked shut. The girl's blood was collected in a pot and then poured over the Countess who sat upright in an armchair permanently installed in the underground chamber.

Bador's self-inflicting sea urchin image chamber tropes Erzsébet's "virgin press," with the exception, of course, that the image of sea urchin harakiri does not imply a victim other than the sea urchin itself. But if we think of "sea urchin harakiri" as a way of processing images, then the world of the past, the migrations and caravans, etc., become Bador's virgins. What runs into the sea urchin's catchment, or better, what this poet pours over us in a gleeful mockery of his aunt's absurd obsession are "cadaver cracks in the lotus pond," "predatory shipwrecks," "a caterpillar laying the droppings of our orphan cries," as well as "decapitated stones," and "mincemeat swarming with scabs."

Here then is an ample selection, the first to be translated and published in English, of the poetry of Bernard Bador. A Frenchman in his early 40s from Lyon, Bador has lived for over a decade in Los Angeles where nearly all of the poems presented here were written. Since Bador has recently begun to write in English,[2] it is quite possible that in the future he will have no need of an American translator.

To make this selection, I have, with Bador's assistance, made a first, literal draft of all of his published poetry (167 poems), as well as over 100 unpublished poems. Based on this initial work, I have completed, on my own, translations of 40 of the 44 poems that make up this book.

Bador's poems in French, more often than not, have only a few words in each line (i.e., he breaks a line where the image "turns," and since thematic possibilities are always being detoured, such "turns" occur frequently). I have found that in English many of the poems come across more forcefully with longer lines, so I have experimented with a number of stanza shapes. I have, however, translated the opening poems in the collection to correspond exactly with the line breaks in the originals.

Several years ago, after meeting Bador in Los Angeles, Robert Kelly wrote the prose poem that the three of us feel is an appropriate gesture with which to end Bernard Bador's American debut.

—Clayton Eshleman,
Los Angeles, November–December, 1982.

14

[1] All the information here on Countess Erzsébet Báthory comes from Valentine Penrose's *The Bloody Countess*, translated from the French by Alexander Trocchi, Calder & Boyars, London (no date given).

[2] Of the 44 poems in this collection, nearly all are from *Le sang du soleil* (1977), *L'hara-kiri des oursins* (1980), and *Sphinx asphyxié* (1984), published by Editions Saint-Germain-des-Prés, Paris. "The Coal Orchid," "The Absent Form the Night," "A Cape of Wild Flies," and "Curdled Skulls" were edited by the translator from drafts written by Bador in English. Eight of the poems translated from the French are previously unpublished.

SEA URCHIN
HARAKIRI

HORS·LA·LOI

Les dés
de l'aurore
ont été jetés
par-dessus
la montagne
des sexes
soumis
au viol impeccable
des parfaits nazis
dans le champ des barbelés.

Les miradors
surveillent
les réclames
abattues
des forêts prisonnières
en marche
vers les balles
de linge souillé
des heures oppressées
des excréments émaciés.

Des cimetières
de lits
flottent
dans
la pâleur des glaces
en océans carbonisés
suspendus
à la rouille
des crochets
de bouchers endimanchés

OUTLAW

The dice
of dawn
have been thrown
over
the mountains
of genitals
subjected to
impeccable rape
by perfect Nazis
in a field of barbed wire.

Watchtowers
guard
the slaughtered
ads
of captive forests
marching
toward hampers
of the soiled underwear
of oppressed hours
of emaciated turds.

Cemeteries
of beds
float
in the icy pallor
like carbonized oceans
hanged
from the rusted
hooks of butchers in their Sunday best

pour la fête
des hordes
d'épileptiques envahisseurs.

Sous
les luminaires
malades
l'infini défilé
des morts
porte
à bout
de rats
les vivants
vers les formules plastifiées
d'astrologues en cage
grillagés
du masque automatique
des reines perdues
porteuses
d'empires
pour tortues en révolte.

for the feast
of the hordes of epileptic invaders.

Under
the sickly
lamps
the infinite procession of the dead
carrying the living
like rats at arm's length
toward the plastified formulas
of astrologers in cages
barred
with the automatic masks
of departed queens
bearers
of empires
for turtles in revolt.

MORT D'UN MONDE

Le vent agite
les cages de fer
suspendues
aux géantes roses amères
des sillages
des lames de sang
à la poursuite
des premiers couchants
d'avant la musique
des feux de lune.

Le miroir se tait
sur les regards
écartelés
entre les sabots enragés
des étalons sans âge
des tremblements de glace
veinée
d'explosions éclatées
à la surface
des alphabets
de mâche-fer.

Les dieux en friche
ont avalé
le verre des houles
d'oiseaux
à la frontière
des plumes rebroussées de silence,
sans force
à la dérive
des expansions bleues
de la mescaline.

DEATH OF A WORLD

The wind agitates
the iron cages
suspended
from gigantic bitter roses
of wakes
of blades of blood
pursuing
the first sunsets
before the music
of moon fires.

The mirror remains silent
on the gazes
drawn and quartered
between the enraged hoofs
of ageless stallions
of quaking ice
veined
with explosions erupting
at the surface
of slag
alphabets.

Fallow gods
have swallowed
the glass of swells
of birds
at the frontier
of the anti-smoothed plumes of silence,
listlessly
adrift
blue mescaline
expansions.

Les sexes taillés
dans les tièdes fontaines
altèrent
les louves
des tribus algébriques
à la cime surhumaine
des abysses des tiges
entre les puissants remous
des chairs
chétives.

The genitals carved
in tepid fountains
parch
the she-wolves
of algebraic tribes
at the superhuman peak
of chasms of stems
between the muscular eddies
of phlegmatic
flesh.

ESSENCE

Dans les frondaisons
du réveil
bleui des serpes secrètes
le sommeil
veille aux spirales d'éclairs
entre les nefs de platine.

Les infirmes
s'agitent
dans les sables mouvants
des coulisses
où se lisent à l'envers
les pulsations inertes.

L'origine
s'achève
au détour des alertes
hurlées sur l'orbite
maladive
des séismes en fuite.

ESSENCE

In the frondescence
of waking
blued by secret meathooks
sleep
holds vigil over lightning
spiraling between platinum naves.

Cripples
toss and turn
in the quicksand
off stage
where inert pulsations
are read upside down.

At the detour of alerts
shouted on the sickly
orbit
of fleeing upheavals
origin
ends.

LA MER

Les crabes apeurés
fauchent les forêts bancales de la Grande Ourse,
et leurs pinces fracturent
le rire en cascade des fresques nautiques.

De molles ramures d'écume
se déchirent avec élégance
contre le surf des rails.

Perfides, les anémones happent,
en douceur,
les nerfs où nichent les lagunes.

Les passants
pressés de rattraper le temps suicidaire,
succombent aux méduses en chaleur.

La mer,
terre inachevée,
roule l'ambre cendré de spasmes humains.

THE SEA

29

Frightened crabs
scythe the wobbly forests of Ursa Major,
their claws fracture
the guffaws of nautical frescoes.

Soft antlers of spume
shred elegantly
against the surf of railways.

Perfidious, the anemones suck in,
ever so gently,
the nerves of nesting lagoons.

Passers-by
hurrying toward suicidal time
succumb to horny medusas.

The sea,
uncompleted earth,
rolls the ash ambergris of human spasms.

Dans l'enfeu des paupières
le gîsant
souffle la corne du sacrifié

Les yeux se dégonflent
saturés de becs bétonnés de froid

Dans la cage
l'espace
se plisse
se déroule
puis se déchire
sous les cris griffus
de nos racines apeurées

Devant vous
le ciel s'enfle et se gonfle
géant
pour avaler le Niagara des morts

THE TRANSPARENT MAN

In the recessed tomb of eyelids,
the recumbent statue honks the crucified's horn.

The eyes deflate, saturated with beaks
concretized by the cold.

Inside the cage, space pleats, unfurls,
then shreds under the claws of roots.

Before your very eyes the sky swells expanding
gigantically to swallow the Niagara of the dead.

« L A R E I N E V E R T E »

à Pierre Henry

Pesanteur du voyage
dans le puits de soi-même
bouché
au confluent sans Messie.

Des cymbales
battent leur plein
sur le pont pourri d'un pubis éventré
à tous les paons

En filigrane
sur la peau du bal
le grésillement des gris-gris grignotés
de grillons de cuivre racornis

Au retors de la bouche,
une pluie de graviers crépite
des étouffements de mousse
sur la porte grinçante des fumées de guirlandes

"THE GREEN QUEEN"

for Pierre Henry

Gravity of the voyage
in the well of itself
blocked
at the confluence without Messiah.

For every peacock
there are cymbals
at full tilt
on the rotted bridge of a disemboweled pubis.

In filagree
on the skin of the masquerade
the crackling of jujus nibbled
by horn-hard copper crickets.

At the rebound of the mouth,
a rain of pebbles patters
moss chokings
on the creaking door of garlanded smoke.

ECHEC

34

Le vent perce l'horizon des morts
entre tes mains trop blanches,
la neige agonise.

La nuit, prise en sursaut,
s'échappe en bramant
par les yeux fixes du grillage

Les barbelés de brume
lacèrent les soleils fauchés
par les naufrages prédateurs

Les faux maîtres d'œuvre
bâtissent des cathédrales vides
pour les danses macabres des rosaces béantes.

Sous tes yeux meurtris,
le sang des raisons s'est figé
en carrières abandonnées

CHECKED

35

The wind pierces the horizon of the dead
between your much too white hands,
the snow is agonizing.

Night, taken by surprise,
escapes belling
through the handcuffed eyes of the grillwork.

Barbed wire entanglements of fog
are lacerating the scythed suns
with predatory shipwrecks.

Fake grand masters
are building empty cathedrals
for the death dances of gaping rose windows.

Under your battered eyes
in abandoned quarries
the blood of reasons coagulates.

SPLEEN

Tout le poids du monde
pendu à une feuille morte
tous les bambous d'hiver
ployés sous la peine du monde.

SPLEEN

The weight of the world
hanging from a dead leaf.
All the winter bamboo
bent under the world's grief.

SUICIDE

Rêve de papillons
striés de rasoirs
foudroiements de phares
à la pointe des lames

Derrière les jardins de sable
le sphinx fossile
maudit les sirènes
le soleil s'est tailladé les veines

SUICIDE

A dream of razor-striped butterflies.
Bolts from lightning houses
at the tips of bladed waves.

Behind gardens of sand
a fossilized sphinx is cursing the Sirens.
The sun has slashed its veins.

MAUVAIS PORT

La nuit s'éventre sur les rocs
et une boue hideuse de goémons
t'emplit la bouche
le sable s'étouffe dans ton for.

Tout a fui, hors le mâche-fer d'âme
accroché à la grue du port gluant
brume des visages en cale sèche
becquetée de hiboux barbus.

EVIL PORT

Night disembowels itself on the rocks,
a hideous wrackish mud is filling your mouth,
the sand is choking in your heart of hearts.

All has fled—except the soul slag
dangling from the gluey harbor's crane,
mist of visages in dry-dock, beakful of bearded owls.

LUTTES

42

La vase suffoque sous les mains
des lunes étrangleuses

Le bleu mouvant de la mer
mobilise les reflets en fuite.

Le sable à coups de frisson
propage les migrations concentrationnaires

Sur les récifs, les cormorans branchus
déchirent l'hypnose de la nuit

STRUGGLES

43

The slime suffocates in the grip of strangler
moons. The sea's moving blue immobilizes

fleeing reflections. The sand, with shiver
clubs, propagates concentration camp

migrations. On the reefs, branchy
cormorants shred the night's hypnosis.

REVES DU CANCER

La sécheresse de rien
ricochets de tumultes sourds
crevés contre
les hauts tambours de lianes

Verts assourdissants
des soleils de boue
lumière de grasse soupe
mangée de mouches roussies

Des crapauds sans mémoire
dans l'attente d'une caravane
au fleuve du couchant
la soif lourde des guillotines

CANCER DREAMS

Dryness of nothing, ricocheting
from tumultous thuds, bursting
against high liana drums.

Deafening greens of suns, of mud.
Light off greasy soup
scarfed by scorched flies.

Toads who cannot even remember
to remember are waiting for a caravan.

In the spreading river of setting sun
guillotines' ponderous thirst.

SABOTAGE

à L.F. Céline

Sous le poids
du linge puant
les piteux platanes
ploient.

Le soir,
les salades suent
l'urine des tubards
en tournée saoule

Les lambeaux de tôle
transpirent à gros relents
les rancœurs rancies
sous les dépouilles

Dans leurs rêves purulents
les petits souillons
sucent
les queues de rats

Sur les vomis en couches
l'air asphyxié
des cris avinés
pèle ses pellicules.

Sans cesse,
les sirènes
sabotent
les suicides
frais plantés.

SABOTAGE

for Céline

Under tons
of putrid laundry
the pitiful plane trees
sag.

In the evening
salad greens sweat
the urine of consumptives
wandering about drunk.

Shreds of corrugated iron
heavily and stalely perspire
a rancor grown rancid
under the spoils.

In their purulent dreams
the slum kids
suck
on rat tails.

On the vomit giving birth
the asphyxiated air
of drunken cries
peels its scurf.

Ceaselessly,
sirens
sabotage
the freshly-sown suicides.

«VOYAGE AU BOUT
DE LA NUIT»

L'homme se ronge
les yeux, le sang et les tripes
devant un petit tas de gros sous
exémeux
qui purulent dans sa peau
d'outre tannée d'or.

La liberté en bronze
lui botte le cul
à coups de grande faim
assouvie dans les poubelles
où pourrit la lumière

Ses rêves sentent le rance
en belles couches épaisses
sur les tartines graveleuses
du port de brumes traînardes
sur la mer mutilée
des cargos prospères.

L'acné des foules
en chômage de vie
suppure sur les étoiles
des décalcomanies délavées
de charnier clos.

Le cosmos crasseux
des culs
envoie ses feux d'hémorroïdes
sur l'orbite
des gravats
de vermines accouplées.

Le soleil trop beau
pour se souiller
dans ce miasme
décharge ses caillots de plomb
dans les égouts
débordant d'avortons.

Au diable les ferrailleurs d'âmes
et les bradeurs de sang!
Mais les nerfs forgent leur calvaire
dans les ghettos de l'avenir.

Man gnaws his eyes, his blood and his bowels
before a tiny pile of fat, eczematous
pennies which pustulate in his hide of
a goatskin bag tanned with gold.

A bronze liberty kicks him in the ass,
blows of terrible hunger satiated
in garbage cans where the light itself
is rotting. And his dreams give off

rancidity like gravel buttered on thick
slices of bread in the harbor of dragging
fog on the mutilated sea of prosperous
cargos. The acne of mobs, disemployed

from life, suppurates on the stars of
washed-out decals of a sealed mass grave.
A cosmic anal filth corruscates
hemorrhoidal light on the rubble orbit

of copulating vermin. And the sun,
too handsome to soil himself in this miasma,
unloads his lead clots into sewers
overflowing with the aborted.

To hell with these scrap soul
merchants, these hucksters of blood!
But the nerves are already forging
their calvary in the future ghettos.

LE JUGEMENT

Harpon
qui ne transperce que les pluies de suie

et puis, les combats de tarantules
dans le trou béant
des abécédaires au sirop.

Tu veux écrire une saga
pour les ébats royaux
de tigres à la fonte des neiges

et ton dernier œil
tombe, vitrifié,
dans la fosse septique.

Le grouillement de lumières,
venin de couleurs,
attire les larves, marée de bave.

Détresse
des solanacées en plastique.

THE JUDGMENT

Harpoon
which pierces only showers of soot

and then, tarantula matches
in the gaping pit
of spelling-books in syrup.

You want to write a saga
on the royal love-making
of tigers in melting snow

and your last eye
falls, vitrified,
into the septic tank.

The wriggling of lights,
venom of colors,
attracts the larvae, tide of drooling.

Distress
of plastic Solanaceae.

LA MAIN

52

Un mur de mouches
s'avance sur les plaies pulpeuses
des fossoyeurs
en pèlerinage aux sources.

Sur l'autel,
où les os se consument
une main gantée d'or
fouille la poussière de la Kabbale
pour étrangler les nombres.

THE HAND

53

A wall of flies
advances across the pulpy sores
of gravediggers
on a pilgrimage to the sources.

On the altar,
where the bones are smoldering,
a hand gloved in gold
paws the Cabalistic dust
in order to strangle the numbers.

54

Scandements roux d'orfraies
accouplés dans l'ivoire d'un miroir limpide

Par les fissures bleues des blessures solaires
l'essor de l'aigle, soudain

Eaux vives des morsures
à même le saut lapidaire du mangeur d'ombres

Dans le jardin de cartes
un cadran de quarts emprisonne
les longues patiences de l'enfance

Russett osprey scannings
mated in the ivory of a limpid
mirror. Through the blue
fissures of solar wounds,
a suddenly soaring eagle.
A spring tide from bites
precisely at the shadow eater's
lapidary leap. In playing-card
garden, a dial of quarter-hours
imprisons the endless
childhood jigsaw patience.

ARCHEOLOGIE

Des quadriges cunéiformes
soulèvent les arches ensablées
des hautes fractures du ciel.

Les inscriptions fleurissent
— jardins insensés —
à l'ombre des éclipses

Ablutions d'histoire
friable poterie
des greniers éventrés d'illusions

La marche solennelle
des statues antiques force
le passage des vaisseaux

Au-delà des paisibles felouques
les glorieuses mythologies
ont rejoint les premiers silex.

ARCHEOLOGY

Cuneiform quadriga lift up sand-entombed
arches of the sky's high fractures.

Inscriptions—like bizarre gardens—
burgeon in the shadow of eclipses.

Ablutions of history, the crumbly pottery
of granaries disemboweled of illusions.

The somber march of ancient statues
forces a passage for vessels. Beyond

the peaceful feluccas, mythological
glories have rejoined the primal silica.

S U R F

Perché sur la crête du surf de lumière
l'homme épouse
la tangente frêle de l'ellipse divine.

La mer glisse sur elle-même
puis s'écarte
de l'appel délirant du soleil

Un torrent d'étoiles abyssales
charrie les royaumes en transit
vers les chutes du silence

Dieu a condamné sa propre naissance
dans cet immense ventre fluide
où agonisent les orgasmes.

Le ressac traîne son ombre
où dorment les volcans
couverts de lotus en bière.

Les dauphins, gardiens du Temple
dansent les calligraphies rituelles
d'avant la mort par les signes

L'approche s'éloigne
sur le sel du mot desséché
une fine poussière de lumière
constelle l'absurde balai des concierges.

SURF

Perched on the crest of the surf of light
man weds the frail tangent of the divine
ellipse. The sea slides on
itself, then recedes from the delirious

calling of the sun. A torrent of abyssal
stars bears transient kingdoms toward
the falls of silence. God has,
in this immense fluid belly where orgasms

agonize, condemned his own birth.
The undertow drags its shadow where
volcanos, covered with lotus caskets,
slumber. Dolphin guardians of the Temple

dance ritual calligraphies before "death by
signs." The approach passes
on the salt of the desiccate word,
dust fine as light

constellates the concierges' absurd broom.

DESTIN

Pourquoi
cours-tu
entre les ronces
des oiseaux migrateurs
vers les équateurs
accouplés
aux passants
pour des guerres
par-delà les temps
du pendule
régulier
matador
aux banderillas
à tire-d'aile
dans les cellules vives
des arènes aveugles ?

Les bulles
de pierre
éclatent
sur le piano
enseveli
sous les bidons de coca
fleurs carnivores
des terres acides
où prospèrent les nains
plaqués
sur les panonceaux bariolés.

Au marché aux puces
des années-lumière
tu trouveras
pour rien

tout plein
de vides trésors
des Aztèques
de demain
le coeur arraché
sous les couteaux
de spirales de lune
à la bouche
des mousquetons.

Les Bouddhas
assoupis
aspirent
les rayons lumineux
au creux
des lobes tendres
cirés
à l'écoute
des nuages de lotus
noyés
dans le sang vieux
des frontières fracassées.

Ecoute les tambours
des planètes
en marche
vers les ellipses
nomades;
le silence
des transhumances
poursuit
sur le sable
les marées souveraines

DESTINY

Why do you run among the brambles of migratory birds
toward equators copulating with passers-by
for wars beyond pendulum-regular matador time
flinging banderillas into the keen cells of blinded arenas?

Stone bubbles are bursting on the piano buried
under coca cans, carnivorous flowers from acidic lands
where dwarfs prosper flattened against garish shopsigns.

At the flea market of light years, you'll find,
for nothing, many empty treasures of the Aztecs of tomorrow,
their hearts torn out by knives of moon spirals
at the baying of the musketoons.

Dozing Buddhas inhale luminous rays
in the hollows of tender lobes stretched
listening intently to lotus clouds
drowning in the old blood of shattered frontiers.

Don't you hear the planet drums
on their way toward nomadic ellipses?

Transhumanic silence follows
the sovereign tides of scenery lying fallow.

Again the universe falls—
unending cascades at the foot of the phantom bird
carved into the foam of secret sails lacerated
under the furious gallop of hordes of wooden horses.

In the distance a caterpillar
nibbling the fireworks at the horizon of parallel
berserk ice floes along the thread of maddened
blades toward the flaming magnet of universal
meetings at the points of pins.

des décors
en friche

L'univers
retombe
cascades infinies
au pied
de l'oiseau fantôme
taillé
dans l'écume
des voiles secrètes
lacérées
sous le galop
furieux
des hordes
de chevaux de bois

Au loin
une chenille
grignote
le feu d'artifice
à l'horizon
des glaces
parallèles
emballées
au fil
des lames folles
vers
l'aimant en feu
des rencontres universelles
à la pointe
des épingles.

LE PECHEUR

64

Il s'en va pêcher le temps
au bout des silences stridents
des striations magnétiques.

La ligne s'est brisée
entre les eaux mort-nées
des cercles jamais assouvis.

Les poissons lents des leurres
relancent leur nage aux heures
fixes du mouvement perpétuel.

Ils sussurrent aux sources
les mystères des cellules mortes
sous les forêts d'invisibles bourreaux.

La masse flotte stérile, vide,
les étoiles ont fui par-delà les rails
vers les cavernes conscientes.

La matière file entre ses sens;
il a pêché l'univers et il sourit réincarné
en suspens au bout de la ligne brisée.

THE FISHERMAN

goes out to cast for time at the end of silent
magnetic striations. Between the stillborn

waters of never to be gratified circles the line
snapped. Slow fishes of lures are again swimming

the fixed hours of perpetual motion. Under forests of
invisible executioners, they are whispering to

springheads about the mysteries of dead cells.
The mass floats, sterile, empty, the stars have fled

over the railroads toward conscious caverns.
Matter slips in through the fisherman's senses.

He has snagged the universe and, suspended in re-
incarnation at the end of his snapped line, smiles.

ODYSSÉE

à Saint-John Perse

La forte mer des citrons
soulève
les nuages verts
des trônes vides
au-dessus des pelotons d'exécution.

Avec le chant des cors
dans les houilles lumineuses
des églises désaffectées
s'enflent tes lèvres
tuméfiées des morsures d'encens.

Ecoute
la poursuite des forêts incendiées
sur les pistes interdites
des exodes
de tes mains liées au cimetière

Il faut abattre
à coups de pubis
sertis de nuées de fièvre,
les longues lianes odorantes
des religions noires.

A toute hâte,
la quille du bateau corsaire
casse la carcasse
des tambours abandonnés
au vent clos des canons.

Je clouerai
à même l'écume des mensonges
le soleil excédé
des tunnels
où tu agonises.

ODYSSEY

to Saint-John Perse

A powerful sea of lemons
is lifting
over the firing-squads
green clouds
of empty thrones.

Your lips tumefied
with incense bites swell
at the blast of hunting horns
in deconsecrated churches'
luminous coal.

Don't you hear
the burned forests being hunted down
on the forbidden trails
of the exoduses
of your cemetery-tied hands?

With pubis blows
set in a cloud of fever
one must fell
the perfumed lianas
of black religions.

Suddenly
the corsair's keel
crashes into the carcass
of drums abandoned
in the cannon-enclosed wind.

At precisely the foam of lies
I will nail up
the exasperated
tunnel sun
in which you lie in agony.

Avez-vous vu les légions d'anges
s'ébattre
comme des sauterelles enrubannées
sur les pyramides des alphabets
en route vers Cygnus?

De chaque côté,
des pieuvres douces
en marche vers les échos des profondeurs,
les murailles retiennent
l'assaut des sécheresses

Toutes les voix
prises en enfilade par les lames lunaires
se déchirent
en silences mous
que seule l'absence trouble.

Plus haut
le regard sacrifié de l'orfèvre
a poli
le miroir incrusté
des folles batailles.

La nef jaune des chamois
a sombré
dans la neige
des calendriers ensevelis
sous les gentianes.

Epaisses fourrures d'Afrique
où s'étouffe
la soif des fétiches
taillés
dans le curare des angoisses.

Laisse le nomade
sculpter
dans ta chair de steppes
l'amphore où verser
les cavalcades des puissants attelages

Have you not seen the legions of angels
falling
like beribboned locusts
over the pyramids of alphabets
as they drift toward Cygnus?

On every side
of the soft octopi
marching toward echoing depths
ramparts check
the droughts' assault.

In flabby silences
that absence alone troubles
every voice
skewered by lunar blades
shreds.

Higher
the sacrificed gaze of the goldsmith
has polished
the insane battle
encrusted mirror.

In the snow of calendars
buried
under gentians
the chamois–
yellow vessel has sunk.

The thirst of fetishes
carved
into the curare of anguish
are choking
in thick African furs.

In your flesh of steppes
let the nomad
sculpt the amphore
into which cavalcades of powerful
four-in-hands are poured.

Sous le règne des grandes rosaces,
obéis
aux invasions des gargouilles chamarrées
de drapeaux des vents poivrés
de Bactriane.

Contemple
à l'envers du houx druidique
les pleines brassées laiteuses
des méditations
des hautes fûtaies de pierres

Sur ta chevelure de jais
les amples migrations des heures
étalent
la brillance des faveurs royales
sur les tatouages des esclaves.

Les caravanes
à l'aube des roses bleues
repartent
vers les paysages de safran
au-delà des gorges crayeuses des aigles insondables.

Après l'exil des fourmis,
tu suis
la chair putride des hyènes
jusqu'à la pestilence
où paissent les ombres.

Ecoute
la danse des grimaces
sur les parois nues de tes peurs
sacrifie ton orgueil
au réveil des menhirs.

Une gigantesque avalanche de silence
broye
l'espace en fuyante croissance
d'atomes bleus, durs et froids,
semences stellaires.

Under the reign of huge rose windows
submit yourself
to the invasions of gargoyles brocaded
with the flags of pungent winds
from Bactriane.

On the backside of druidic mistletoe
contemplate
the milky armfuls
of meditations
of soaring rock forests.

On your jet-black hair
vast migrations of hours
are spreading over
the brilliance of royal favors
on the tattoos of slaves.

Caravans
move out
in the blue rose of dawn
toward saffron landscapes beyond
the gypsum found in fathomless eagles' throats.

After the exile of the ants
you follow
the putrid hyena flesh
as far as the pestilence
in which shadows graze.

Don't you hear
the dance of grimaces
on the bare walls of your fears
sacrifice your pride
to the waking of menhirs?

A gigantic avalanche of silence
crushes
space into a fleeing expansion
of blue atoms, hard and cold
stellar seeds.

APOCALYPSE

Des fous
plongent leur rage
dans une sueur de pleurs
et les temples saccagés
rejettent les momies
dans l'ignorance de l'hiver

Des masques de sciure
dansent
entre les bambous blancs
du festival de la peur
sur les airs transis
des toundras reniées.

En bordure d'équilibre
l'étrange tourne
sa géante girouette
tabou de l'espace
où claquent
les bannières du gel

Les grillages de lune
ont accroché les plumes lourdes
des sources disparues
aux sourds tambours
des roches grises.

La nuit
tranche le sang des tortues affolées
dans les rapides entonnoirs
des aubes glacées
des ailleurs électriques.

A plein vent
sous les drapeaux
tendus pour les joutes sans dames
les chevaux se lancent
sur les bouffons roides.

Le soleil des mers rebelles
a cerclé
le terne étendard
du phoenix moissonné
dans le vif-argent des ossuaires.

APOCALYPSE

73

Madmen plunge their rage into a sweat of tears
while plundered temples cast out their mummies
    into the ignorance of winter.

Masks of sawdust dance between the white bamboo
    at "the festival of fear"
to the bone-chilling airs of the denied tundra.

    On the edge of equilibrium
the strange veers its weather vane, a space
taboo, where frost banners are flapping.

The moon's wire meshes have hooked
the heavy feathers of disappeared springheads to
    the deaf drums of grey rocks.

Night slices the blood of turtles stampeded
through the swift funnels of icy dawns.

Exposed to the wind under flags set out for jousts
    without ladies
steeds surge down upon the stiffened buffoons.

A rebellious marine sun has encircled
the lifeless standard of the harvested phoenix
    in the quicksilver of ossuaries.

NAISSANCE

Grosses de mouches,
des chamelles cherchent les fissures
à facettes.

O puits faussaires
des os en semence !

Grands prêtres,
descendants initiés de l'impuissance,
remballez les graffiti des liturgies
payables à domicile.

Mieux vaut trouer l'air
qu'inciser les bulbes
de croix à carrefour aveugle.

Apre,
une épave de rose écorche la seconde,
blessure de lumière
sur le mandala fané d'yeux en cendres.

Derrière,
s'échappe un long cri mauve
dont l'aigu a tranché le biruti pétrifié.

Mort-nées, les mouches
s'abattent
sur la peau des vestales voilées.

Accrocher
âme
mur.

BIRTH

Camels pregnant
with flies searching for facetted
fissures.

O forger wells
of bones gone to seed!

High priests
initiated into impotency
pack up the graffiti of C.O.D.
liturgies.

Better to make a hole in the air
than at a blind intersection
to core the bulbs of the Cross.

Acrid,
a spar of rose wreckage skims the second,
a wound of light
on the faded mandala of eyes in ashes.

Behind all this,
a long mauve cry is escaping,
its high note has sliced the petrified biruti.

Stillborn, flies
are swarming
the skin of veiled Vestals.

Soul
hookable
wall.

LE PROGRES

Aveuglements de jacarandas
rehaussés des lourdes cymbales de l'été.

La mélodie s'en va mourir
sous le laminoir des doryphores,
ardents époux des myosotis.

Sous les flashs,
les nourrissons sans visage
écorchent les danseuses.

Mutisme trouble des aras
écartelés sur la roue des focs
gonflés de morsures d'ours.

Tristan Tzara foule le puits sacré
des saturnies
fauchées par les coupe-coupe.

A l'appel des termites-totems,
les murènes guède
commencent la ponte des marées,
grelots éclatés
sous la levée des sables héraldiques.

O le charisme des déluges !
Corps-à-corps des boues turgescentes
où s'enfoncent
les défenses des morses asphyxiés.

PROGRESS

Jacaranda blindings
heightened by summer's ponderous cymbals.

The melody slinks off to die
under a rolling-mill of potato bugs,
ardent myosoti spouses.

Under the flashings,
faceless sucklings
are flaying the dancers.

The turbulent macaw mutism
is quartered on a wheel of main-jibs
swollen with bear bites.

Tristan Tzara tramples the sacred wells
of the peacock butterflies
scythed by shamrock machetes.

At the call of the termite totems,
pastel blue moray eels
begin to lay tides,
popping sleigh-bells
under the murmuring of heraldic sables.

Ah charisma of deluges!
Hand-to-hand of turgescent mud
into which asphyxiated
walruses are plunging their tusks.

ANABASE

Les nuits de cuir
galopent dans le champ des visages.
O fouets de cris
sur les croupes foudroyantes !
Par les semences de sueur,
le pavot couronne le ciel.

Le grand gel des prières
se mire dans l'écho des crevasses,
étalons de marbre et de bronze
chargent le vent des défaites.

Confins des lois
gardées de neiges apprises,
algèbre de sable
dans les yeux trop verts
des coursiers captifs de Kara Koroum.

Il faut franchir le gué
des cerfs-volants incolores,
pavillons pirates
sur les roses de mer.

L'automne des nuages
—miel de verre soufflé—
brouille l'adieu des sculptures.
Musées de chair
livrés au prisme des géométries.

Un parfum de griffes
flotte sur l'éclipse des lèvres,
sang lacéré des lunes
sur le granit des retours.

A N A B A S I S

Leather nights are galloping in the field of faces
O whips of screams
on thundering rumps!
By sweat sowings the poppy crowns the sky.

A vast frost of prayers
is admiring itself in the echo of crevices,
bronze and marble stallions
are charging the wind of defeats.

Confines of laws
guarded by instructed snows,
algebraic sand
in the bright green eyes
of charger captives from Kara Koroum.

One must wade across the river
of colorless stag-beetles,
Jolly Rogers
raised on marine roses.

The cloud-lit autumn
—honey of blown glass—
blurs the farewell of the sculptures.
Museums of flesh
delivered to the prism of geometry.

Claw perfume
floating about on the eclipse of lips,
blood scraped from moons
on the granite of returns.

Des mains couvertes de bagues
caressent les palmes roses,
odalisques de soleil sur la couche fraîche
des feux de la nuit.

De sveltes éphèbes
encensent l'abîme des sources du ciel,
sur les tapis de soie,
l'épée partage les mondes antiques.

Les courtisans se donnent à la mer
et leurs mains de marbre
brassent les massives noyades.
O morts des demi-saisons !

Les yeux en friche
profanent l'herbe jaunie des marches,
ombres séchées des palais,
enceintes rousses des béantes brûlures.

Face à face,
les invasions de rage
enfouies dans les fourrures de fleurs
et l'épais velours du sang.

Dans les triples coupes d'or,
les mangoustans, papayes et goyaves attendent
les pur sang
laqués de poussière conquise.

Hands covered with rings are caressing the pink palm trees,
odalisques of sun on the fresh bed of night fire.

Svelte ephebes
are incensing the abyss of the sources of the sky,
on silken carpets
a sword divides the ancient worlds.

Courtesans are abandoning themselves to the sea,
their marble hands are churning up massive drownings.
O you dead of the between-seasons!

Fallow eyes
profane the yellowing grass of strolls,
dried up palace shadows,
rusted enclosures of yawning burns.

Face to face the invasions of rage
buried in flower fur
and the thick velvets of the blood.

In flaring gold chalices,
mangoes, papayas, and guavas await
the thoroughbreds lacquered with conquered dust.

RENAISSANCE

Le soleil s'achève
dans la fontaine des tablas,
dentelle de joyaux chamarrés d'os
rouillés sous l'iode ivre des idoles.

Sous l'appel des lavandes,
le doute encercle les crépuscules migrateurs,
mutilations sereines d'avant le port.

De Varanasi à Jahangira,
un sadou hypnotise le Gange,
paralysie de fleurs et parfums de crémation
à la vue des charognards imberbes.

La terre glisse
entre les dents des dieux,
cornes d'abondance.

Naufragé,
rouvre la grille forgée d'anémones,
sang tentaculaire des ablutions de lune.

A l'ombre d'un point,
le troisième oeil rougeoie,
amande amère égarée dans la neige.

Vivant cryptogramme
des cavernes à flanc d'oiseaux
condamnés aux frigides vertiges des cascades.

Comment rompre le rideau des yeux?
Abandon d'une main sacrilège
sur le phallus aigu des résines durcies.

CADAVER CRACKS IN THE LOTUS POND

The sun concludes
in the fountain of tablas,
a lacework of gems bedizened with bones
rusting under the drunken iodine of the idols.

At the call of the lavenders,
doubt encircles the migratory dusks,
serene mutilations before the port.

From Varanasi to Jahangira
a sadhu hypnotizes the Ganges,
a paralysis of flowers and cremation scents
in view of beardless carrion eaters.

The earth slips
between the fangs of the gods,
horns of plenty,

Drowned man,
reopen the wrought anemone gate,
a tentacular blood of lunar ablutions.

In the shadow of a dot,
the third eye reddens,
an acrid almond wandering the snow.

A living cryptogram
of caverns on the flanks of birds
condemned to the frigid vertigo of cascades.

How break this curtain of eyes?
Abandon of a sacrilegious hand
on the pointed phallus of hardened resins.

Brisures de cadavres
sur l'étang de lotus,
flottaison de cris entre les lobes d'or.

Le volcan a pétrifié l'encens femelle
d'un sourire,
accouplements d'entrailles millénaires
mûries dans le silence apprivoisé.

Une main nouvelle
soulève l'horizon à hauteur de crinière.
O le galop des pôles!

La souffrance voûte les orties
privées de cathédrales,
mais qui se souvient des rugueuses acanthes
du zodiaque, lèpre de faussaire
ou péage des galaxies?

Entre deux éternités,
un garuda rutilant encourage
l'éléphant oublieux de la forêt.

Courbé d'or inutile,
le grand prêtre des images condamne
le culte des neiges,
squelette borgne des avortements de Kabbale.

Tortures avides de sons,
herbier griffé des sommeils en feu,
sous les braises,
une rose dévore le phaccochère.
O safari des oraisons jaculatoires!

A point,
la lune, torsade d'harpes vertes,
libère la foudre suave,
frénésie des scarabées transparents.

Cadaver cracks
in the lotus pond,
cries floating the golden lobes.

The volcano has petrified the female incense of a smile,
couplings of millennial entrails
ripened in the tamed silence.

A new hand
lifts the horizon up mane-high.
Ah the galloping of the poles!

Suffering stoops the nettles
deprived of cathedrals,
but who recalls the rugose acanthi
of the zodiac, a forger's leprosy
or a galaxy toll-booth?

Between two eternities
a rutilant garuda encourages
the elephant who has forgotten the forest.

Weighed down under useless gold,
the high priest of images condemns
the snow cult,
a one-eyed skeleton of Cabalistic abortions.

Tortures greedy for sounds,
a herbarium raked by sleep on fire,
under the embers
a rose is devouring the wart hog.
O safari of ejaculatory prayers!

In the nick
of time, the moon, a torque of green harps,
liberates the suave thunderbolt,
a delirium of transparent scarabs.

BIOGRAPHIE

Dans la mer moisie des fouilles,
le pollen dissout les œufs du ciel.

Entre les murs du rail,
les miroirs embrouillent la rage des escarbilles.

Sous la rouille des étamines,
les yeux se cachent après le mauvais amour des houles plates.

Sur le tambour,
une voix s'échoue au bord du message.

O mots déchiquetés
d'avant le dictionnaire périmé des heures!

Sinuosités du sang
piégées dans l'écriture des crocs.

Des requiems alourdis de crapauds
bloquent l'essor des veines.

Sourires saturés de mouches
aux crochets du boucher.

Dans l'antre purulente,
le nouveau-né torture l'ombre de l'air.

BIOGRAPHY

In the moldy sea of excavations,
the pollen dissolves the eggs of the sky.

Between the railway walls,
mirrors confuse the rage of clinkers.

Under the rust of stamens,
eyes are hiding behind the vile love of flat swells.

On the drum,
a voice stranded at the edge of a message.

O words shredded
before the out-dated dictionary of hours!

Sinuosities of the blood
snared in the writing of fangs.

Requiems weighed down by toads
blocking the soaring of the veins.

Smiles saturated with flies
on butcher hooks.

In a purulent den,
the newborn child tortures the shadow of the air.

DESTIN

Du sang caillé
dans le bol du vent,
et dans le cahier
l'agonie d'un enfant.

DESTINY

Blood diarrheal
in the bowl of the wind,
and in the diary
a child's agony.

L'écriture,
rivée à la grille
du cauchemar.

Ossements d'âme
jonchés sur les brumes
où veillent les amarres.

A l'aube des voeux,
la souplesse de la neige,
l'Inti Rami
investit le coca sans paupières.

Schizophrène,
un serpent encercle les montagnes,
symboles avortés
des lourdes insoumissions.

Alors, au creux de l'aile,
poind
l'or de l'ascension,
cicatrice ciselée dans la pénombre.

Writing
riveted to the night-
mare gate.

Skeletons of a soul
littering the mist
where hawsers keep watch.

At the dawn of vows,
the pliability of the snow,
Inti Rami
lays siege to the eyelidless coca.

Schizophrenic,
a snake encircles the mountains,
aborted symbols
of ponderous insubordinations.

Then, in the wing's pit,
the gold of the ascension
peeps through,
a cicatrix chiseled in the penumbra.

EMPLOI DU TEMPS

La mer se retire
au-delà des faisceaux d'œufs lézardés,
pavanes de sommeil
sur l'écume noire
des carapaces de sable.

Soulevance massive
de secondes prématurées,
cibles trop grêles
même pour les javelots pétrifiés
des fleurs carnivores.

D'énormes tortues
couvertes d'yeux de brume,
gravent de rituelles douleurs
sur les mandalas d'algues rauques.

Vengeur,
un cormoran unijambiste
—despote d'îles pubères—
étripe
à coups de bec à répétition
le pélican avaleur de vierges.

Un typhon,
tourbillon de siècles,
en grande paix intérieure,
repose
sur les lèvres mangeuses d'hommes.

DAILY ROUTINE

The sea withdraws
beyond the bundles of cracked eggs,
pavanes of sleep
on the black spume
of sandy carapaces.

A massive upheaval
of premature seconds,
targets too fragile
even for the petrified javelins
of carnivorous flowers.

Enormous turtles
speckled with eyes of fog,
engraving ritual pains
into the mandalas of raucous seaweed.

In revenge,
a one-legged cormorant
—the despot of pubescent isles—
guts
at machine-gun-beak-fire
the pelican swallower of virgins.

A typhoon,
the tourbillion of centuries,
with a grand inner calm,
reposes
on the man-eater lips.

LES QUATRE SAISONS
DE LA NUIT

Poissons assassinés,
doctes assemblées en nage,
pourquoi ne pas emprisonner
les reflets des faucilles faussaires?

Si le foin s'en mêle,
il ne restera plus aux meules qu'à gerber.

Dans les vomissures,
les Indiens del Norte de Mexico
engendrent les expansions gamma.

Un champignon s'interroge,
turgescence de velours,
tandis que les fantômes de Cythère
lèvent l'ancre de l'âme.

L'émiettement des mers recouvre le vent,
et tous les officiants s'éternisent,
brûlés par le fiel des ophiures.

Eclipse de poissons-lunes
dans la coquille céleste et dans l'œil,
une écharde d'étoile
fait sourdre la lame obscure.

O les quatre saisons de la nuit!

THE FOUR SEASONS OF THE NIGHT

Assassinated fish,
learned assemblies bathed in sweat,
why not imprison
the reflections of sickle forgers?

If the hay butts in,
the stacks have no alternative but to throw up.

In the vomit,
Indians from the north of Mexico
are breeding gamma expansions.

A mushroom questions itself,
in a velvet turgescence,
while the phantoms of Cythera
draw up the soul's anchor.

Crumbling seas cover the wind,
and all the officiants eternalize,
burned by the gall of ophiuroids.

Eclipse of fish-moons
in the celestial shell and in the eye,
a star shard
makes an obscure tear well.

Ah, the four seasons of the night!

LA DECOUVERTE

96

Fourmis schizophrènes
du Grand-Oeuvre
en percée de montagnes.

En deçà,
vibrent les falots
des isolés en marche forcée.

Pourtant, dans l'aube noire,
nous retrouvons la fissure savante
où se sont glissés les dauphins.

Dans le creuset,
l'œil enfin géant et solitaire
pour les bougies inutiles.

THE DISCOVERY

Schizophrenic ants
of the Great Work
penetrating mountains.

Over here,
vibrating, the lanterns
of the isolated on forced march.

Nevertheless, in the black dawn,
we recover the wise fissure
into which dolphins are slipping.

In the crucible,
the eye at last gigantic and alone
for the useless candles.

L'APPEL DES
CAVERNES

Menstrues de tapir,
jouissance
pour les fourmis bleues
rescapées
d'un rut abortif
le soir où
la lune s'est pendue
aux langues
suceuses
de chattes enneigées.

Béat
comme une nuée enceinte,
le cyclope
droit,
le membre chargé,
s'aveugle
d'huile vaginale
que sillonne
l'ovule des mondes.

Dans une poche
intestinale,
le mangeur d'opium
étend
le drap des fleurs cramoisies
sur le grondement rocailleux
des laissés pour compte
du radeau
de la Méduse
livrée
au calme paralytique
des spasmes crépusculaires.

Une bande d'oursins
en prière
dans le jardin de pierre
perce
le mystère des bâtons,
assassins
perce-oreilles
logés
sous la mousse
des crânes,
sépultures
de musiques
muettes.

Un kleenex
essuie
l'ampleur des vagues,
froissure royale
pour cueillir
le miel des yeux
extracteurs de chimères
sevrées
de traîtres scorpions.

Un fleuve
s'engourdit,
gelée maligne
des sorcières d'épicerie
semécs
aux quatre peurs
de la foire des hommes,
mais les cafards,
ignorent-ils

CALL OF THE CAVERNS

Taper menses, an orgasm
for the blue ants rescued
from an abortive rutting the evening when
the moon hanged itself from snow-
capped pussy sucker tongues.

Inanely happy like a pregnant cloud,
the erect cyclops, his member loaded,
blinds himself with the vaginal oil
that furrows the ovule of worlds.

In an intestinal pocket,
the opium eater unfurls
the sheet of crimson flowers onto the rock-like rumbling
of rejects on the raft
of the Medusa abandoned to
the paralytic calm of crepuscular spasms.

A band of sea urchins praying
in a stone garden penetrate
the mystery of rods, killer
ear wigs lodged
under skull moss,
sepultures of mute musics.

A kleenex wipes
the amplitude of waves, a royal crumple
to dab out the eyes' honey
extractors of chimeres weaned from traitor scorpions.

leurs bourreaux
victimes
de défectueuses strates?

Collier de têtes,
balanciers de la torpeur
des transfusions souterraines
où les syphons
étranglent la lumière,
l'agonie
d'un bison
—tornade de boyaux
et bêlements
de chasseurs hébétés—
a révélé
la communion
des gravures
dans le grain du rocher.

A river becomes numb,
malicious jelly of grocery witches
sewn at the four fears
of the fair of all men, but the cockroaches,
do they—victims of defective strata—
ignore their executioners?

A necklace of heads, pendulums of the torpor
of subterranean transfusions where sumps
throttle the light, the agony
of a bison—tornado of entrails
and bellowings of stupified hunters—
has revealed the communion
of engravings in the rock's grain.

IMPUISSANCE

Juste une chanson
avant la marée rouge
balayeuse de prunelles,
miniatures de chaotiques genèses.

Mais que peuvent musique et paroles
sur l'enceinte pourrissante
de nos mains aveugles,
tâtonnant entre les foetus,
pullulante peuplade cannibale
sur la pelade du ciel?

Du pont, surveilles-tu
l'eau trouble,
hachis grouillant de croûtes,
scrofules amoureuses
de tendres cous?

Homme bandé
sur un croissant de lune,
supplie l'invisible archer
de couper les liens d'Hadès
et de suivre la flèche de feu.

Mais sur le miroir de la nuit,
seul,
le reflet fané d'une rengaine,
vomissures de gargouilles
astrophages.

IMPOTENCE

Just a song facing the red tide
sweeper of pupils, miniatures of chaotic geneses.

But what can music and lyrics do
on the rotting enclosing-wall
of our blind hands,
groping through the foetuses,
a pullulating cannibal people
on the alopecia areata of the sky?

From the bridge, are you keeping watch on
the troubled water,
a mincemeat swarming with scabs,
scrofula in heat
for tender necks?

A man stretched taut
across a crescent moon
begs the invisible archer
to cut his ties to Hades,
to let him follow the arrow of fire.

But on the mirror of the night,
alone,
the faded reflection of a catch-phrase,
vomitings of astrophagous gargoyles.

Une pierre sculptée,
intense,
écoute,
décapitée,
les rouages souples
d'une saga en sanscrit.

Mais qu'importe la langue
quand le sang
se tapit
dans la clairière.
O le guet des méditations en crue!

Chavirements en cale sèche
pour cet oiseau
sans aile,
migrateur
au dedans de soi-même,
soif des voix invisibles.

Toujours,
la lune obsédante,
caravane sans maître,
lents méandres sous les paupières
qui s'effeuillent
sur les arbres rouges,
être absent.

Les anneléides
ôsent danser
et leurs métamères
emportent
les momies
après le mauvais banquet

où la mer s'étouffa
de retour du vomitorium.

Un choeur supplie le vent,
germination gémillipare
dans le grain du marbre,
le sourire fantôme
déclanche
l'apocalypse
pour les éponges en croix.

SECRET ENTABLATURE

A sculpted stone, intense,
listens, decapitated, to
the flexing gears of a Sanskrit saga.

But what use is language when the blood
hides in the clearing.
O vigil of floods of meditations!

Capsizings in dry dock for this bird
without wings, a migrator
within himself, a thirst for invisible voices.

Always, the obsessive moon,
masterless caravan, slow meanderings under eyelids
that loose their leaves onto red trees, absent being.

The annelids dare to dance
and their metameres carry off
the mummies after the vile feast where the sea

choked to death upon returning from the vomitorium.
A chorus beseeches the wind, a gemilliparous germination
in the grain of marble, for the crucified sponges

a phantom apocalypse-triggering smile.

CHASSE ROYALE

Derrière le mur
des vomissements
de salamandres
arc-boutées
contre les cactus,
sadiques écorcheurs
de mini-nuages,
angelots bouffis
d'un cerveau
assoiffé de phénix,
cendres multicolores
en marche molle
vers les horloges
trébuchantes.

Un crotale
secoue le sorcier,
amulette immobile
sur la corde rocheuse,
file de faux rêves,
avarie de voyages
à bout de souffle
dans les gares
éraillées des insomnies.

Une nuée de vers,
glu velue,
pour la récolte
des crottes syncopées,
mais l'air,
brûlure d'ange,
roule
contre les tambours

en rupture de tympan,
ivresse gothique
sous les flamboyants
en position de lotus;
l'orage d'un bâton
sur la nuque
pliée
à contretemps.

Tirée
sur nulle neige,
la troïka
fait vibrer
la mue rigide
des fractures
foetales.

Dans l'iris,
l'œuf de la licorne,
Confucius
au loup de bambou,
trace
sur les larves
le tunnel
des grottes de plein air
où s'égarent les dédales,
inventions
de lutins
couverts de caillots frais
pour repousser les éclairs,
moelleux miroirs
où s'impriment
les faces

ROYAL HUNT

Behind the wall of vomitings of salamanders arched
against cacti, sadistic flayers of mini-clouds,
puffed up brain cherubs thirsty for a phoenix,
multicolor ashes on a flabby march toward stumbling clocks.

A rattler shakes the charmer, a motionless amulet
on the rock-like rope, file of false dreams,
breakdown of journeys out of breath
in railroad stations husky from insomnia.

A cloud of worms, hairy bird-lime for the harvesting of
syncopated turds, but the air, angel smut,
rolls against the drums at odds with tympanum,
Gothic drunkenness beneath the flamboyants in lotus position;
the storm of a baton on the nape folded against the beat.

Drawn across no snow
the troika makes the stiffened
moulting of the foetal
fractures vibrate.

In the iris, the unicorn's egg, Confucius in a bamboo
half mask, traces on the larvae the tunnel of open
air caves where the mazes become lost, imp inventions
covered with fresh clottings to push back the lightning,
marrowy mirrors where the forger faces of
the triangles are imprinted, altars of repose
for the eye, ah mystery of the shell!

The sphinx—an obsession of cells in which worlds are whirling—
absorbs all the formulas, excrement of brainless ants,
and on the lips, runways, the daft smile of Mona Lisa,
a sow escaped from pig bristles.

faussaires
des triangles,
reposoirs de l'œil.
O mystère de la coquille!

Le Sphinx
—obsession de cellules
où tournoient les mondes—
absorbe
toutes les formules,
excréments
de fourmis écervelées,
et sur les lèvres,
pistes d'envol,
le sourire benêt
de Mona Lisa,
femelle échappée
de soies porcines.

Encerclements
de soi,
prisons de coupures,
ruées railleuses
des alphabets
sans feu,
ni lettres,
ni roue,
ni femme.
O primitif traqueur
des vaisseaux spatiaux,
verroteries
d'idéogrammes
où s'étiolent
les chasses hardies
brisées
sur les strates,
tassements de cavernes
asphyxiant les sphères
sommes de musiques imsomniaques!

Self-encirclements, prisons of cuts, scoffing
onslaughts of alphabets without fire, nor letters,
nor wheels, nor women. Ah primitive
flusher of space ships, beaded glass ideograms
where daring hunts etiolate, broken on the strata,
settlings of caverns asphyxiating
the spherical sums of insomniac musics!

DIPTYQUE

Sur la taie d'oreiller,
le sable
du squelette rêveur
et l'eau morte de nos peaux,
décor mâché
par des myriades de scolopendres,
blattes, blabères et cancrelats bijumeaux,
confluent
avec toute la sûre lenteur des bulldozers
vers les bouches insonores.

A côté,
le porteur d'eau des poissons
filtre la cadmie rectale
où nichent les larves-étoiles
des matins chauds
quand le soleil
fige les papillons
sur les orbites creuses.

O la nouvelle éclosion des iris!

DIPTYCH

On the pillowcase,
the sand
of the skeleton dreamer
and the stagnant water of our skin,
a scenery gnawed
by myriads of scolopendras,
water-bugs, blattids, and four-headed cockroaches,
converge
with all the slow sureness of bulldozers
approaching sound-proof mouths.

Nearby,
the fish-water bearer
filters the rectal cadmia
where the star-larvae of warm
mornings nestle
when the sun
pins the butterflies
to hollow orbits.

O the new blossoming of irises!

AUX CANNIBALES

L'envoûtement d'un crâne
où boire la fin du monde
diluée dans le sirop épais
d'un sang souillé
de blancs d'yeux globuleux.

Tu voulais y graver
le relief des astres,
carcasses anonymes
fomenteuses de miasmes.

Vaine fut l'émission rauque
des vieux crapauds
avaleurs de lunes,
le langage créa Babel et Hadès.

Faute de foi,
les cannibales n'ont rien résolu,
il eût fallu se consommer
jusqu'au dernier !

TO THE CANNIBALS

The bewitchment of a skull
out of which to drink the end of the world
diluted by the thick syrup
of a blood stained
by the globular whites of eyes.

There you wanted to engrave
a relief of stars,
anonymous carcasses
fomenters of miasmas.

In vain the raucous emission
of old moon
swallowing toads,
language has created Babel and Hades.

For want of faith,
the cannibals have resolved nothing,
the last ones would have had
to consume each other!

The following four poems were written in English alone.

115

In our empty bladders the vampire winds roar

Swathes of thrashed bat wings
lie in drifts

THE ABSENT FROM THE NIGHT

Leaf eaters
dead under man's breath
unhook
the moon
bullet ridden
by pregnant flies

Into the uteral ponds slide
the pilgrim penises,
tectonic coital thrusts
of emerging darkness

On the vault
the star scales illuminate
the swimming of the signs.

A CAPE OF WILD FLIES

Beyond the silent aurochs-haunted forests,
victims give birth to victims,
white she-wolf jaws crush
the black lord's

epileptic sleigh on the powdery
sand of summer, sand
promised to the horse blood drinkers.
The multiple odyssey under each step!

A hardened rainbow shelters the tarot players
whose fauve oil faces long to crush
the trembling she-mummies
scratching at the surfaceless sheer walls.

Bloodsplashed palettes of eyes.
The fine nerves we entangle in concrete clouds.
After all, the moon does
menstruate on the shadows of our limp

members and bonzai willows dot
the weary fur of our retinas.
Her eyelids hung with deadly nightshade
stuffed bats, her sheets

wet with the blood of virgins,
the royal harpy again and again
yields to peaty crusades of orgasms.
The juice of marine snails

germinated on Uranus streams
from the sex of icy stones
while witches from the Karpaths
anoint the Countess's vaginal chasm.

In the darkness of underground wash houses,
hordes of infuriated, trilobite-fringed
fledglings immerse themselves in the storm graffiti
chiselled in our limestone lungs.

CURDLED SKULLS

The butcher debones the violets
with a suckling's love
for the alpine breast
scattered with curdled skulls

*

At the sprouting of the first bud
a blue shriek of saws
which the madness of the rake would have liked
to twist around its little prongs

*

Sound attacked from every side,
codfish rotting in the beds of bishops
mossy with canonical butts

*

In the flower bed
a slug is urinating on a masochistic spider

*

Obese women with very delicate joints
dragging about bloated snarling cats
packed with porcupine quills

*

Tongues vibrating
in the tops of bald trees
fish shadows teeming
with schools of men

*

Out of breath but smooth with semen
milky spiders
forage in our troubled eyes

*

The bird comes into you through your eyes
ripping out in beakfuls
the tender shoots of your steps

*

Sounds shelled on a rosary of barbed wire

*

In the night of curdled eyes
caterpillars
lay
the droppings of our orphan cries

*

Choked under the mourning caramel
mobs bury themselves
with velvety yells

*

Covered with antique snow
the pollen of our draw-bridge languages

*

Music hanged itself
from a tumefied tongue
in search of an echo
a fly paces up and down

*

An orchestra conductor in tears
elevates to fire's limits
the lacquered veins of luminous winds

    *

The sun longs for gravedigging waves
but shivers at the sweet swift swish
of the multicolored harp of razors

    *

A capillary breath
marinated in embrace's smut
irrigates
the aurora of the living disguised as the UnDead

FIN DE PROMENADE

A Makiko

Carnaval d'âmes rouillées
en quête d'huile de lune
pour lubrifier cet engrenage de l'œil
enterré sous les mousses métalliques.
Un piano briseur de notes
mène rondement
cette diarrhée d'ombres disjointes,
taches asséchées
où grouillent,
paillettes papuleuses,
les œufs des pythonisses
aux seins gonflés de lait caillé.
Leur secret désir
reste de sevrer les ranatres,
masse grignoteuse
des petits du soleil tuberculeux,
rejetons, orphelins d'âme
jetés à la rocaille
des oracles,
raclures scrofuleuses
des yeux de verre.
Les vents s'y étouffent,
noyade attisée par la mauvaise haleine
des chèvres
déféquant des montagnes de crottes.
Odyssée du Guano d'or.
Te souviens-tu des sirènes
voleuses de pies
vierges de tout nuage?
Il eût fallu les écouter;
rochers dentelés de la chair
des victimes extatiques
où peut-on vous retrouver?

END OF THE WALK

To Makiko

Carnival of rusted souls in search of moon
oil to lubricate this eye gear
buried under metallic moss. A note
breaking piano leads, briskly,
this diarrhea of disjointed shadows,
dried up stains where papulous sequins,
the eggs of pythonesses, their breasts
swollen with curdled milk, are teeming.
Their secret desire remains: to sever
the bedbugs, that nibbling mass of tubercular
sun babies, off-springs, soul-orphans
flung to the rocks of oracles,
scrofulous peelings off eyes of glass.
Winds are choking there, a drowning
fanned by the bad breath of goats
defecating mountains of droppings
The Odyssey of Golden Guano.
Do you recall the sirens, those magpie
thieves, free of every cloud? One should
have listened to them; jagged
rocks of the flesh of ecstatic
victims—where can we find you?
Our wobbly incantatory dances raise
a dust of stingings in rut. Ah the titanic
wasp nest engulfer of the shipwreck of
the very last islets of refuge for
tentacle men! Painful contortions for a mere
drop of cervical sap. Bubbles
popping at the inert surface. Nothingness
wandering the deserter void of amnesiac
amnions sabering—to the blows of a scramasax—
a gluey colony of scolopendras, the question mark's
gaseous compositions of jealous gusts.

Nos danses incantatoires bancales
soulèvent une poussière
de dards en rut.
O le guépier titanique
engloutisseur du naufrage
des ultimes îlots-refuges
d'hommes tentacules!
Douloureuses contorsions
pour une goutte de sève cervicale.
La crevaison des bulles
à la surface inerte.
Le néant déambule
dans le vide déserteur
des amnios amnésiques
sabrant à coups de scramasaxe
la gluante colonie des scolopendres,
bouffées jalouses
des décompositions gazeuses
du point d'interrogation.

POSTFACE

Prose pour un Lendemain

by Robert Kelly

The Countess Erzsébet Báthory (Liz) lived in a language half-way between Hungary and New York. I love her though she was very cruel. She drank the blood of her lovers, and exposed servant girls naked in her snowy courtyard and watched while their robust pinkness turned redder then paler then finally livid. It is interesting that she liked to look at naked women, and that her glance was so dangerous. It hurts people to look at them, the way she and I do. I have been told my eyes burn when I look at people, and I have been likened more than once to a Siberian mink, yes, that's true too, but monk is what I mean, a monk of a later time, one who is still alive, it may be, and singeing dark impressionable gentle-women with the fervor of his glance. His glance misses nothing. But enough of me. Consider Báthory Erzsébet (as they say in Magyar), Liz, she was a mink too, always at it, sexual to a fault, glossy with desire, a pornosopher-queen, keeping fealty to the lordly impulse that (whether from angel or devil) ran her frantic life. Being in bed with her must have been like being in bed with an orchestra, and not a decorous *hofkapelle* of the time, but a roaring sweating turn of the century magnum of an orchestra, pounding out a Sacre du Printemps or squeezing the last seminal juices from a Verklaerte Nacht. I think of Liz, in the grip of her wild music, turning her penknives and needles and ice-cubes on herself when all other victims were away at church or kept from her by officious major-domos in the pay of her brother the king. I think of her tears of pain and quiver of sheer unfocussed sexuality as drops of blood squeeze out of her pierced thigh; she is just as pink, tender, innocent in the flesh as any of her victims. It makes no difference. She makes the body speak, theirs, her own. She challenges its innocence, challenges its capacity to rouse feeling and be roused. With her lovers she arouses them and herself by the spectacle of wounded girls, wounded boys, and those victims too must have survived or died in some rapt mingling of sensuality and dread half a world's literature has tried to record and decode. The pain of love! Who knew it better than Liz, a slavic literalist, a magyar mystic, a catholic metaphorist, a diabolic enthusiast, all her skills to the one question. And that question is a linguistic one, perhaps: what is the word of the body? What is the word of which blood and semen and lymph and vaginal juices are the syllables spelt slowly by the pressure of flesh, at the prodding of steel, cold, heat, wet? I honor her inquiry still: we live in it, we move in it, it seems to be us, seems to carry us wherever there is to go. But what is it, this body, this luscious flesh that time impeaches, *what is it in itself?* Make it speak its name. Like all interrogators, Báthory Erzsébet ultimately relied on torture, *la question.* She too would die under the torturers, and men would fancy that a condign punishment. I think of her dying in orgasm under their screws and rough hempen ropes, the only torture is that her body will speak its word only a moment after she has lost the capacity to hear it, only when she has left the lewd hotel of her flesh and found her naked soul sprawling in the dark of a more than Transylvanian night. Hoofbeats in the wild night, wind, no moon, but some vestigial glow behind the driven cloud wrack, romance, terror and no au revoir. Perhaps she stands near us when clumsily we jab needles in our fingers or burn our hands on hot panhandles, or watches us whenever the sexual moment comes. Would we recognize her if, in one of those sudden astral snapshots that whirl through the mind of a lover coming, we suddenly saw a woman we had never seen before, her sculpted lips parted as if to catch word or come? Cold and regal and detached she was painted by the lubricious symbolist Csök Istvan (who moved to Paris and became Etienne Csök), cold in her furs as the poor serving girl is cold in her naked submission to the invisible torture of the weather. That's how they wanted to see things in the Paris salon—all mood and no mayhem—Géricault and all that was well in the angry past. Perhaps the French were right—hold victim and torturer in one careful composition of color and suggestivity, the tension of her burning eyes only to be inferred, and always to be inferred. It is unFrench of me to see so much blood around Liz, and disrespectful thus to the French branch of her family, les Bathory, who in the thumbscrew of time found their name shortened, made more French. My friend Bernard Bador is of that clan, and I speak with him often about his admirable handsome sexy wicked old aunt Liz, *la louve sanglante.*

—Robert Kelly 11/13/80

The first edition of this book consists of one thousand copies. Twenty-five clothbound copies are signed and numbered by the author, translator, and author of the postface. Each of these twenty-five has an original tipped-in collage by the author. An additional twenty-five clothbound copies are signed and numbered by author, translator, and author of the postface. Twenty-six clothbound copies, in an edition *Hors Commerce*, are lettered A–Z.

The text was typeset in Goudy Oldstyle, and printed on acid-free paper.